NURSES RETURN TO NSR

How to navigate successfully in a stressful work environment.

LORETTA L. BONNICK, RN

The opinions expressed in this manuscript are solely the opinions of the author and do not represent the opinions or thoughts of the publisher. The author has represented and warranted full ownership and/or legal right to publish all the materials in this book.

Nurses Return to NSR
How to navigate successfully in a stressful work environment.
All Rights Reserved.
Copyright © 2015 Loretta L. Bonnick, RN
v4.0

Cover Photo © 2015 Loretta L. Bonnick, RN. All rights reserved - used with permission.

This book may not be reproduced, transmitted, or stored in whole or in part by any means, including graphic, electronic, or mechanical without the express written consent of the publisher except in the case of brief quotations embodied in critical articles and reviews.

Bonnick Press

ISBN: 978-09910443-0-6

PRINTED IN THE UNITED STATES OF AMERICA

Dedicated to Michael:
My soul mate, who is perpetually supportive of all my ideas and goals.

Our children, Michael Jr., Joseph, Jacob, and Kate:
always ushering me towards a new perspective on life.

Table of Contents

Preface vii

Chapter 1: You Can Change Your Job Situation 1
Unity of Mind 1
Why Am I Attracted to This Career? 3
Thoughts and Feelings 5

Chapter 2: Reclaiming Your Power 7
Make Your Day into That Which You Desire 10
Closing the Day 14
A Simple Meditation for Unwinding 15
The Magic of Sleep 16

**Chapter 3: Forgiveness—The Art of Cleansing
Oneself/One's World** 20
Let Go of Dead Things 22
Embrace Freedom 23
Perseverance, the Passage to Resolution 24
Accept the "Cleaner Fish" in Your Life 25
Divine Order Aligns Your Outcome 27
Write to an Angel Sometimes! 29
Thank the Angel for the Healing of the Situation: 29

Chapter 4: The Law of Nonresistance 31
   No Person Can Deny Your Good! 35
   Add Honey to seemingly Lemon Situations 37

Chapter 5: My Words Are My Destiny 39
   Heal Self First 39

Chapter 6: You Are Not Alone 43
   Affirmations 44
   Why I Wrote This Book 47

References 49

Preface

This book is based on my experiences of practicing as a Registered Nurse in various institutions. It brings to one's attention the practical application of living and surviving a career field which is not always based on team support. It is meant for individuals who enjoy their career and get challenged by their passion to care. There are many biblical citations, as the Bible was a source of reference for metaphors used as an application to living. The references are not meant for any religious purposes; rather, they are used in the light of their pragmatic and spiritual applications.

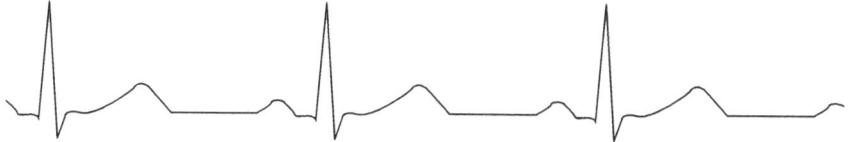

Chapter 1

You Can Change Your Job Situation

Does your job seem overwhelming? The new staff schedule dictates that you work with less, but produce the same outcome. Do you sometimes think that after all these years of studying that your patients think that your job description is merely to empty bedpans and remove their empty trays? Do patients and doctors speak to you condescendingly? Nothing seems to be going right for you anymore. Management seems helpless because everyone seems to be in the survival mode, concerned for his or her own best interest, meeting the bottom line, and maintaining whatever it takes to keep the paychecks coming. You feel alone, and maybe even trapped; the elation of the career seemingly has lost its savor. The career of vanilla ice cream with caramel topping now tastes like bitter lemons. What can you do to restore sanity? The monsters of this nightmare are closing in to swallow you up. No one can fix this situation but you. It sounds crazy, but it is true. We control our environment, consciously or subconsciously, in every action that you participate in or every word spoken.

Unity of Mind

There are three departments that controls our mind in its daily functions, creating the results of our daily experiences and activities. They are sometimes referred to as the "Trinity." The conscious state (Son), subconscious state (Holy Ghost), and the superconscious state (Father). The conscious state is our objective world like the thoughts we think and the emotions we feel about the experiences we encounter daily. The conscious mind is the way we view life. It is the way we characterize things, such as sickness, sadness, health, joy, limitations of any kind, and abundance. This is the information that is impressed on our subconscious mind.

The subconscious replicates the information that it receives. We can equate this to a rubber-stamping process. The subconscious does not have the power to change itself, it regurgitates the image transmitted from the conscious mind. The subconscious cannot take a joke. Joking around with negative statements, such as, "I am sick and tired of things," ushers you into unhappy experiences."For whatsoever a man soweth, that shall he also reap."

The superconscious is the perfect state of man. It is that part of you that triggers your attention to those desires that you think are unattainable. The superconscious is the guiding light of man that directs his purpose and destiny. The superconscious is the Divine Intelligence ingrained inside every cell of the human body, constantly nudging one to self-actualization."I press towards the mark for the prize of the higher calling." We have the power to change our situations to make them ideal for our existence. It is now that we have to find the Divine source within to heal us. This Divine Intelligence/Source has the power to unchain us from years of negative thinking, entrapment, ushering us to our right place in life. This only occurs when we start thinking and acting in a different way in anticipation of a better outcome.

Why Am I Attracted to This Career?

You decided to join up with the healthcare career, maybe because a nurse was an inspiration to you or a relative was an integral influence on your career choice. You may have been inspired because of a traumatic event in your life, and in enduring the traumatic event, you decided to spend the rest of your life caring for others. If you have the passion for working in the health industry, for the love of saving lives, giving enlightenment to others, educating and counseling your fellowman, then you are on the right trajectory for purpose and destiny.. The reward of this is the satisfaction of seeing that your work contributed to the greater good of humankind, by improving the quality of life in others. In the quest of contributing to the greater good, there are challenges or detrimental factors that would hinder you from a productive, prosperous life. If you entered the career as a means of getting wealthy, then you will quickly realize that you will become a consumable resource for amassing this wealth. The harder you work, the quicker the burn-out. You have become like the proverbial candle in the wind. It is now time to re-evaluate your value system.

True wealth and prosperity is being at peace with oneself and one's vocation, finding joy in what you do. In likeness, the universe will bountifully reward you with all the goods, services, and pleasures that your heart desires. You may notice that there are people who amass many material items, yet have no peace, and they spend a lifetime in pursuit of that one thing that will balance their life path with the vibration of the universe. In other words, getting up every day and doing that thing that brings joy to the soul. It does not matter if upon appearance, your co-workers seem as if they came from hell, nurse managers with horns on wheels, or an institution that has a work environment likened to a labor camp. These seemingly unbearable situations are part of your creative process, on the path to your soul's growth. We created such environments to propel us to our greater good. You may start disagreeing upon hearing this, but you will understand better as we continue on this journey together. Sure, you can reclaim your happiness, restore hope within yourself, and create a work environment that is pleasurable to work in. Of course, it takes work and discipline of the mind. Together, we will work to change our minds (thoughts) and change our lives. No need to be running to change your jobs. The change begins within. **When the inward man's concepts of self have changed, it allows for his world around him to synchronize with his thoughts.**

In the process of changing our world, we must practice replacement of the negative thoughts with positive thoughts. We must practice daily affirmations; these are statements of truth regarding a situation producing the likely outcome anticipated. Understanding that thoughts are things, they come to life. *Man is the artist who paints the masterpiece of his life by the thoughts he daily ponders.* In practicing affirmations of truth, one should rid self of gossip, negative thoughts, and negative people around one's environment. Do you remember the times at the nursing station when the discussion was about the challenging patient that no one wanted for his or her assignment, or the doctor who everyone thought he/she did not know his or her scope of practice? Do you recall those seemingly anxious relatives who wanted to stand over you for every procedure that you had to perform for the patient on the unit? Remember when you had requested your day off for that special occasion weeks ahead of time, and the wonderful nurse manager ignored it, put you on the schedule anyway, and said, "Deal with it!" Did this incident cause you to start on the negative trail? Does this sound like a challenge? You may respond by saying yes, because it is perfectly normal to gravitate towards the negative of any given situation. You may think it is unrealistic, but take a moment and start thinking about conversations that you participated in, and later on, you discovered that the negative thoughts you entertained had now become likely happenings in your own life. Coincidence? Not likely. Whatever you give attention to will grace you with its presence. You attract to yourself that which you think and feel emotionally. The emotional feeling regarding that thing is what we create. We are a part of the creative process of life.

Thoughts and Feelings

Thinking (Intention) + Feelings(Expectations) =Creation(Experience).

The time is now. It is now time to stop doing and saying the same things in our daily lives that we do not desire, and expect different results. I have met nurses with ailments of all sorts. They constantly speak of the difficulties of their illnesses. They tell you that they expect to get better, but proclaim the wrong results. They declare statements such as, "I don't think I'll ever get over this," or "I have to take this medication for life," or "I hope to be better someday." The reality is that one will not subconsciously attract health and wellness by proclaiming negative statements or thoughts contrary to one's true desires. "Death and life are in the power of the tongue." Constantly speaking of a situation in the negative perpetuates its growth. It is like pouring fertilizer on plants. They get bigger and produce an abundance of the crop planted. Do not expect to reap tomatoes when you planted corns. Say, what you mean, and mean what you say. Speak only the best for each challenge. It does not matter what others say or what the environment around you predicts to be the likely outcome. Affirm every situation good. Declare everything good. Our change starts by identifying that we are the catalyst for the change we seek. Will there be a cavalry of doctors, a bevy of administrative officials, or a group of unions or nursing associations to bring the change that you desire? I must share this with you. They will *not* be the rescue team for your woes. Did you notice that after working 5, 10, 15, or 30-plus years things have not changed? Sometimes it seemingly gets worse with seniority. Here, you may have younger managers as your boss whom you believe do not give you the respect that you rightfully deserve. Now that you believe condescension has been served out to you, assert yourself in the posture of leadership. Interpret the speech as the other person speaking up to you. Respond as a leader yourself and not as a subject of ridicule or indignation. **If you do not celebrate yourself, no one else will celebrate you.** It is time to get out of the land of make-believe and stand in the posture of taking full responsibility for the occurrences in your daily life. See and feel yourself in the light of what you deserve, and see others equally in their mutual positions in peace and harmony. By thinking and seeing outcomes in this positive manner, you will not have the inner fear of thinking that someone is going take what belongs to you neither will you think that you have to destroy others to get ahead.

Now that we have recognized that we create our world, we must understand that there is a Divine Creative Force/Universal Life Source or intelligence that dwells within us that will guide us to our true place in life.

Affirmation

Universal Life Source guides me to my destined purpose in life. I am confident as peace surrounds me in all areas of my life. Universal Life Source sustains me in all that I do. Goodness now pours into my life as I open myself to receiving from Universal Life Source.

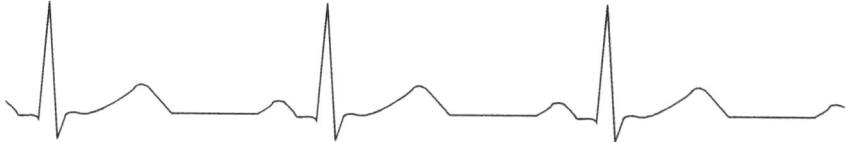

Chapter 2

Reclaiming Your Power

No one is ever powerless in any given situation. To change our world, it begins with you. The first step is to take responsibility for the things that are happening around you. Today, your day starts with a bang! It seems as if you belong to everyone else but you. As soon as you receive your report for the day, meds are due, every doctor seems to be rounding at the same time, new orders need to be picked up, patients need to go for CT Scans, (Computerized Tomography) and you can't locate the transport aid or a PCA/CNA (Patient Care Advocate /Certified Nurse Assistant) to help. One of your patients is climbing over the bedrail, and another has C-Diff (Clostridium Difficile) stool running over the bed to the floor. A family member wants your full attention to fluff the pillow of their relative, not concerned that you have other patients on the priority list of critical issues. Having this awesome workload, you must be able to stand in the midst of it all and not lose face. The patient is expecting a smile, and pleasant disposition with each contact. The doctors require a professional response regarding questions asked about your assigned patients. In addition, your nurse manager is taking notes on your reaction, and your evaluation day is coming up. This is not the time to scream, curse, or become a raving beast.

How did you prepare yourself for this day? It is not a hate assignment; what did you meditate on prior to this banquet? Alternatively, what new height have you been challenging yourself to embrace? Find the lesson in this situation. **Neither personality nor circumstance is your adversary. In the classroom of life, the student learns from every teacher.** Take a deep breath and exhale. It is now time to go within and commune with your friend and life partner, spirit man. Now is not the time to start whining, complaining, cursing, or venting bile on anyone. **When you continuously vocalize the events, you create more of the same situation,** *as your subconscious state creates for you that which is your focus of attention*. Your subconscious goes "to prepare a place for you . . . I will come again and receive you unto myself . . . where I am, there ye may be also". Your subconscious will only create what you gave to it from your conscious daily activities and exchanges. Your attitude towards situations make them heaven or hell. Heaven and hell are states of mind by one's attitude and reaction towards situations and events. Think positively, speak positively, create solutions concerning your troubling situation and the outcome will be the desired result which is heaven. Think, speak, and act negatively about the situation on hand and the results will be more tormenting events (hell) "If I ascend up into heaven (thinking ideally), thou art with me; if I make my bed in hell (thinking negatively), thou art with me."

The subconscious state accepts all thoughts as it is always with you. The subconscious state creatively processes our thoughts every second of every minute of every day and night. Contemplate the Divine presence within and give thanks for the guidance. Divine Guidance will give you the strength and create the help you need to meet your goals. You will find that your mind will become calm and still and you then will be able to focus appropriately.

In the midst of the chaos, start picturing the opposite of what is happening. Changes may not happen immediately, but keep

RECLAIMING YOUR POWER

that picture within. It keeps you calm and focused. The changes will come. Infinite intelligence is ready and waiting to execute your smallest and greatest demand. Every thought is a desire, spoken or unspoken, and it is a demand made to our subconscious or the Divine Intelligence dwelling within. Our subconscious always answers the demand made upon it. Delivery may come in a moment or later. ("Acquaint now thyself with him, and be at peace; thereby good shall come unto thee.")"Him," referred here, is the Divine presence within you who is ready, willing, and able to strengthen you and change your situation to that which you desire."Peace be within thy walls and prosperity within thy palaces."

Recognizing that Divine presence dwells within you, things will be moving in your favor. You will be at peace because you now recognize that you are not alone. In embracing the Divine presence, your world now changes and the prosperity of divinity regarding your moment now becomes a manifesto. Being in a relaxed, calm state of mind allows you to think logically and handle situations without intimidation and fear. I remember being on duty in the ICU one night, with six patients, four on a ventilator, and one patient is on hourly finger stick, no PCA(patient care aid), and the ER is calling for admissions. One staff member called in, the nursing office had no replacement, and there were only two RNs on duty. The incoming staff panicked, but in my mind, I saw adequate staffing and calm everywhere. After the buzz was over, we asked the ER to give us an hour with the admissions. The nurse supervisor was later able to supply another RN and a PCA(patient care aid) for help, and then we were able to discharge one of our patients to a less-critical floor. It always works out. Stay calm and trust Divinity to guide you. Divinity promises to "never leave you or forsake you."

LORETTA L. BONNICK, RN

Make Your Day into That Which You Desire

Start your day by communicating with your Divine Self. No one is more important than you are. Your world is for you to enjoy, and events happening should be pleasing for you. "You," here, is not the pompous egoist, but egoism in recognizing that the Divine presence dwells within. The Spirit within will guide you to think and speak right about things, producing the right outcome of events. Here is where the writer of Philippians said, "Whatsoever things are true . . . honest . . . just . . . pure . . . lovely . . . good report, if there be any virtue, any praise, think on these things." If you find yourself constantly speaking negative of a situation, you can immediately declare to yourself "*cancel,*" or denial of the thought or word spoken by declaring, **"No!, or I only accept that which is good in this experience.** " Quickly replace the negative with an equal exchange of a more desirous outcome. It is just like voiding a check after writing an incorrect entry. The beauty of thinking the right outcome and speaking graciously concerning others and situations is that what you give to others, you also reserve for yourself or you can look at it as interest made on a deposit. As you speak and think well of others, the same returns to you and your situation. Lift your spirits by affirming, **"Good is everywhere and in all things. I gladly accept the good in all experiences."** Encouraging yourself in this belief system will attract to you positive outcomes.

Upon awakening in the morning or evening, before you rush into the day ahead, take some time to write your script for the day. **We are playwrights, life is a script, and we have become the actors in the play.** You now have the choice to write your own script and decide how you want it read. You also decide the actors and the role each will play in the game of life. Plan for your day that no matter what comes head-on, it will be a part of your plan and no mountain will be high enough to keep you away from your good.

RECLAIMING YOUR POWER

Find yourself a quiet place to start your day/night. You are now in the mode of prayer. Prayer is the ability to believe what the five senses have denied. It changes our outlook, hence, our expectations will change our countenance. In quieting ourselves, we are now dimming the activities of the objective senses, like turning the lights down in the theatre before the movie starts. Our mind is now passive, and we will feed into it information that we require to change our situations. We adopt the emotion (feeling) of that desired state; we are now in the process of reversing unacceptable actions into situations of likened desires. "Thou shalt decree a thing and it shall be established unto thee." Do not be concerned with provision of the need. Your only duty is to stay in the wish fulfilled, see completion. Do not try to find ways to work things out. Infinite Intelligence/Universal Life Source has ways, which you know nothing of, and it is the purpose of Infinite Intelligence/Universal Life Source to give you your heart's desire.

Breathe peacefully and deeply and watch your exhalations. Inhale and exhale to the count of four. Repeat until you feel calm and peacefulness around you and in you. In the midst of trying to focus your thoughts, you may find your body starts complaining and your mind starts telling you about a million things that needs doing, and how much you need to hurry because you have limited time. The competition now starts on who should get your attention, mind, or body? You should never hurry your way through life. Hurrying breeds anxiety, stress, and wrong decision-making. At the time of getting quiet with self, symptoms of pain, shivering, cramps, upset stomach, itching, hunger, or any other physiological problem may announce themselves. This is your body trying to get some attention from you. It has become jealous that the mind is always directing you and getting your attention. This is now the time to calm the storm.

LORETTA L. BONNICK, RN

Let us start with quieting the body first, as we will later need to project our minds into the ideal of our day/night. Start affirming, **"I now unwind and release everything and everyone that hampers my path to progress. Peace envelopes my being and harmony clothes my world."** Start relaxing your body, starting from your feet to your head. Feel and see each body part completely relaxed, then start blessing your body from organs to cells. Your feet represents your understanding; therefore, you are transmitting the message of calm to the mind.

Praise the body for the great job it does for you every day, how it keeps you strong and protected. You will now notice that it will be much easier to start your affirmations for the day. Your body is like a child in tantrum who will not stop stomping until you give attention to the exhibition. Set your day by stating, **"This day/night is successful, I am happy, and blessed. I see only good things happening because Divine Life Source is with me . I am capable of overcoming all obstacles, because Divine Life Source gives me strength. Good comes from this day, because Divine Life Source surrounds me wherever I go. All things are possible and I can do all things because Divine Life Source strengthens me."** Repeat this as many times as necessary until you feel convinced or peaceful that this day is set in motion for you. You can spend from 5 to 15 minutes preparing yourself, longer too, PRN, (as needed).

The day contains endless lessons to learn, and infinite blessings packaged just for you. Make sure that you have clearly defined within yourself that which you truly desire. Create pictures of your day, the way you would like to see things unfold. Put your camera in motion and run the script. Speaking your mind with those difficult staff members before proceeding to work with them. Bless

RECLAIMING YOUR POWER

them and congratulate them on how meaningful they are to you. Bless your patients, decree health for them. In decreeing prayers of blessings, see your seemingly enemies receive great blessings. As you bless your enemies, known or unknown, they will become enchanted and magnetized to your good or eventually fade away from your world."The rain falls on the just and the unjust";"bless and curse not." The blessings that you give to others are the blessings you give to yourself .Have meaningful conversations in your mind; hear those you speak with respond to you in words that you want to hear."Therefore, I say unto you, what things so ever ye desire, when ye pray, believe that ye have received them, and ye shall have them."

We telepathically transmit thoughts of concern to those we think about without their conscious approval. If accepted, these thoughts will influence their behavior. What you emotionally feel of someone else kindles those feelings in that person. What kind of fire are you building before starting your day? Is it an out of control forest inferno or a controlled flame of love and joy? Make things amicable before you enter the workplace. Your world will not change until you have changed your ideas of it. Go into your day expecting the best, counting all the little blessings and decree that everything is good, no matter what the picture looks like. When you start taking time to pray and put things into perspective, things usually get worse before they get better. It is like cleaning out a clogged drain. In the cleaning process, malodorous sludge flows down before water flows freely again.

You cannot believe everything you hear or see around you. In the decision to change your world, one of your greatest challenges will be your five senses. Your five senses will always cause the truth to elude you, transfixing you to the illusion of your present circumstances. They will direct you to intellectual facts of reason in an attempt to deny your imagination of its creative power. **"Imagination is life to the changes you seek",** for as oxygen is to the red blood cells, so necessary is imagination to your existence. You cannot change your circumstances without it. There can be no outer change until it is pictured within. Outward actions do not create the change you need. Outward actions are only temporary fixes. ***The pictures we create in imagination, and accept as truth about ourselves creates the changes in our outer world.*** Futility is struggling to change circumstances around you before changing the picture in your mind. Change in situations occurs only after you have vacated the current state and dwell in the new picture or desire in the mind.

If you find yourself on a sinking ship, it is time to abandon the voyage. There is a lifeboat called "imagination." Imagination is your ability to create a new life, molded in the way you desire it to be. Are fixtures of institutional regulations written in stone? They appear to distill your imagination and keep you frozen in the belief of impossibilities dictated in your world. You will find that your every working hour will have you operating as a mechanical robot, chained to the belief system of another. Unchain your imagination. No one really has the power to steal your desired good from you unless you give them permission. Imagination is a private world for you, and Divine Intelligence within will create whatever you can conceive."Pray to thy Father in secret and thy Father which seeth in secret shall reward thee openly."You have the power to re-create your heart's desire and live your life to the fullest.

Closing the Day

The adrenalin high is over and it is now time to cool down. The day's/night's events are on a picture slide in your mind. You are sorting through your mind looking at how things could have turned out differently. You found out that you literally took your patients home with you when you started thinking about their symptoms. Here is where you start feeling sorry for the patient. Is he/she going to make it to the next day? At this moment, you have started the creative process of injecting their diagnosis in your own life. Replace the feeling of sorrow with thoughts of health and peace, instead of absorbing the sorrows of the one in need. Flashes of the medication charting comes to you. Did I sign off on all meds and nurses' notes? Tossing and turning like the restless sea, unable to sleep, it is now time to revise the day and bring closure to your thoughts. **Man is the artist painting a masterpiece of his life daily by the thoughts he continuously entertains.** "Keep thy heart with all diligence, because out of it are the issues of life." As you did in starting your day/night, relax your body and mind.

A Simple Meditation for Unwinding

Create a space for unwinding the day/night. This could be in your bathtub while bathing, a closet, an easy chair, or anywhere you can be alone for 5–15 minutes, longer if your environment allows. *You can incorporate music, candles, and pleasant smells. It is your environment, and you decide what helps you to become relaxed.*

1. Place yourself in a lying or sitting position that allows your back to be straight and is comfortable to you.

2. Watch your chest moving up and down. With each exhalation, start counting from 1 up to 4. Keep repeating until your body starts feeling relaxed.

   Or . . .

1. Start relaxing your body beginning with the toes. Speak to each member of the body by stating, "I let go. Peace and tranquility envelopes me." "You should then continue starting with your toes, moving upwards to the feet, legs, all the way up to the top of the head".

2. Close your eyes and imagine that you are floating like the clouds way up in the sky on a bright sunny day.

Once this peaceful state is established, you can now revisit your day, starting the moment you wake up. Anything that was unpleasant to you throughout the course of the day, **mentally re-create the events of the day so they become conformed to your expectations.** They could be conversations with coworkers, patients, and relatives, or letters with unpleasant news. You should mentally alter the facts of your life, as it breaks generational curses of constant reoccurrence of the same, moving you into active creation of the ideal state. **Life is as a book: daily review and revise to change the ending of the story.**

The Magic of Sleep

After putting to rest the activities of the day, it is in sleep that we have the marriage of the conscious and subconscious mind; your thoughts will now become things. All of your words and feelings will merge as one as your physical body goes to sleep. The conscious mind is the bridegroom, and the subconscious mind the bride. The bride beckons the bridegroom to be one with her. "Rise up, my fair one, and come away." Like the bride, the subconscious mind awaits to absorb the thoughts of the conscious state, all our conversations, and emotions about people, places, and things. Earlier, we learned that this bride does not argue, neither does she try to change the

RECLAIMING YOUR POWER

bridegroom. She receives the seed given to her and processes it in a likely manner out picturing the seed thought form in our world. The children (circumstances and activities) we have running around in our world, dramatic, unfamiliar, and mind-boggling, as they seem are our reproductions of the union between conscious and subconscious thoughts taken to bed as we sleep. The Children, created in our image and likeness, are a reflection of us "in his own likeness, after his image." The thoughts that you embraced at night is as a fertilized ovum implanting itself in the walls of the uterus for growth. This thought greets the subconscious state for reproduction.

While your conscious state is asleep, the subconscious is busy toiling to bring to pass the request it was given."He that keepeth Israel shall neither slumber nor sleep." It behooves you to assume feelings of happiness, success, health, and prosperity before sleeping."Enter into his gates with thanksgiving and into his courts with praise" affirming, "I am happy,""I am successful,""I am healthy,""I am prosperous,""I am complete." The subconscious is the perfect bride who waits to gratify her groom (conscious mind). "My beloved is mine and I am his, By night on my bed I sought him whom my soul loves, I found him whom my soul loves, I held him and would not let him go ." It is the bride's pleasure to birth the children of conscious desire. Whatever thoughts or feelings you lingered on throughout the waking hours will now manifest as actions in your world. Therefore, turn away from the sad appearances of the day, leave the land of regret. Hold close to yourself feelings of the moment in the state you wish them to be."He calls those things which be as though they were."

Whatever is your desire, the superconscious state initiates a preview of your greater self by giving you the desire. Divinity in you makes it achievable. **"Desire is only unattained success"**. Induce yourself to the state desired to attain that which you hunger and thirst for. **A desire becomes mature when you fill yourself with feelings of fulfillment that the need is already met.** Your day will be determined by the mood that you last imprinted on the subconscious state prior to sleeping. "Whatsoever ye bind on earth will be bound in heaven . . . loose on earth will be loosed in heaven." Thoughts and emotions, conceived on earth (our material plain where our ideas are created, i.e., conscious thoughts), becomes shapes and expressions in heaven (your subconscious thoughts), which are events that unveils in your waking hours. You have the power to determine the outcome of your world; it is yours by divine right. You have the power to manipulate it for changes and control it to produce the likely outcome.

Use your power wisely. The world around you cannot change unless you change from within. In our daily interactions with life, we are as farmers gathering seeds in the fall to prepare for the next planting season. We gather seeds and nuts (thoughts) everyday in our experiences. Planting of seeds begins indoors in the winter, and then is transferred outdoors in the spring. We have a winter season every time we go to sleep (rest). The state of mind that lingers with us before sleep is a seed retrieved from our fall gatherings. The harvest we receive in spring/summer depends on the type and quality of seed we planted. Our subconscious, like the earth, receives all seeds planted. When the winter has passed (awakening to your activities), spring and summer comes. Everything is in full bloom (daily exchanges and encounters, good or unpleasant). The seed (thought) planted in winter/spring will now produce plants and fruits in great abundance. Choose your seeds and nuts wisely. Make them become . . . "health to thy navel and marrow to your bones." Collect only those that are healthy, nutritious, and beneficial.

RECLAIMING YOUR POWER

You have the power to decide what enters and exits in your world. As on a cold winter day, when you wrap yourself in a thick wool blanket, so should you engulf yourself in thoughts of idealism. Postulate yourself always with happy resolves. Like being in love, enamor and consort your desire, then embrace, entertain, and permeate the desired state of fulfillment and completion.

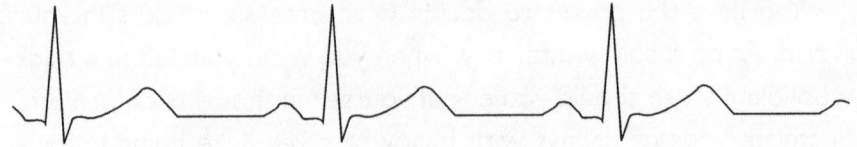

Chapter 3

Forgiveness—The Art of Cleansing Oneself/ One's World

Our outcome equals our input. We have to take responsibility for our daily encounters. The Law of Forgiveness allows exposure to your subconscious state to provide a harmonious environment through the act of imagination and declaration of truths regarding your situation. The Law of Forgiveness is defined as "The process of releasing the acknowledged offense or infringement imposed by the offender. Forgiveness is not for the sole benefit of the offender but for the purpose of releasing the forgiver". It allows one to free oneself from a hostage situation in the mind. We hold others hostage in our minds because of what they said or did to us. We become possessive of persons, places, and things when we clutch them emotionally in our minds, because we cannot seem to find a place for forgiveness. When we clutch on to the seemingly offense by another, one then begins the process of creating a world of similar experiences. This process delays our success and prosperity. The process of unforgiveness starts with daily meditating on the negative behavior vented towards us. We talk about it to others and as we do, the re-enactment of the event continues. With each reenactment, the anger within increases. This usually leads to the daily

FORGIVENESS—THE ART OF CLEANSING ONESELF/ONE'S WORLD

visualization on how to manipulate the offender's behavior to gain control of the situation or get even. This creates blockage in our subconscious, hindering our soul growth and expansion in life. The law of forgiveness frees us and the concerned situation or person into each likely good. As we daily speak words of release from the situation, we impregnate the release of emotional possession held subconsciously. Freedom to all configures one's heart's desires, propelling one into purpose daily. The thing that works is one's ability to reverse the incorrect thinking towards people, places, and things. The way the law works with forgiveness is that one has to abandon critical negating thoughts, discharging oneself from thoughts of bitterness and fear.

Did you ever work with that one nurse or subsets of nurses who smiles nicely with you and the moment you step across the room; she/he, they have the worse things possible to say about you? Not only do they speak evil about you to your coworkers, but they also make an appointment with the nurse manager to give an induction into their "hall of evil" regarding your performance or general disposition. You often find out about this after being reprimanded or later receiving a low performance review. Your co-workers, feeding from the negative news spread about by this one or group of vicious person/s, avoids you as they become prejudgment about you. What do you do in this situation? Thoughts swirl in your head of wanting to get even with the person/s, avoiding this individual or group, telling everyone how evil they were, or sometimes even wanting to confront them head-on. Do not try to figure out what seemingly went wrong. Now is the time to get in touch with the divinity within, forgive the person/s who appears to have transgressed against you, and ask their forgiveness inwardly for thinking angry thoughts when you discovered they had supposedly wronged you.

Asking forgiveness of the person/s is clearing yourself of any baggage that would later manifest as similar happenings around you or clinical disorders taking residence in your physical body. Now, you are thinking that this is indeed, the passive approach. Earlier, I spoke of sending out negative thoughts about others. Here is what happens. If someone sends negative thoughts or deeds to another, and the one intended does not accept this as the truth of their world, like return mail, the negative thoughts have to return to the sender, which would be you, the initiator of the thought. This can be summed up as "Whatsoever a man sows, so shall he reap." This is why we should implant forgiveness in every situation as the wise prophet stated, "Forgive our debts as we forgive our debtors."

Let Go of Dead Things

Keep yourself clean of stagnant, unproductive thoughts. Clearing oneself of negative clutter allows for the creation of an inner vacuum. The creation of the subconscious vacuum relieves one of possessiveness. When you are angry with someone, you have allowed that person to possess and control you. What do I mean? If someone has done something that you believe is an offense to you, do you find that you change direction when walking down the same path? Do you avoid verbal exchanges? Do you constantly think of the person with an emotion of hatred or anger? When making up your work schedule, do you make sure that you do not work on the same day/night they are scheduled? Does he/she drive you to believe that you should consider transferring out into another area of work? Do you flat-out avoid them as much as possible? If you have identified with these characteristics, then you have given over your power to another, by allowing him/her to possess you. One should never allow others to control one's emotions.

FORGIVENESS—THE ART OF CLEANSING ONESELF/ONE'S WORLD

What is the truth that you believe in? If you are not sure what to believe in, then this is when you need to spend some time giving thanks to Divine Intelligence for the wonderful creation called by your name. Give thanks that you are in your purpose and destiny to contribute to the greater good of humanity. It does not matter if your name does not flash in neon lights; your existence is purpose and destiny. Like roots of a tree, the tree depends on the roots to supply needed nutrients for its continued growth. Therefore, you should see yourself as an intricate part of the healing process endowed with the necessary skills, grace, and knowledge for this moment, at this location, to enhance and affect the lives entrusted to your care. You are fulfilling your destiny in soul growth by the vocation chosen.

***Prayer of Affirmation:** Infinite love in me greets the infinite love in all people around me. Infinite love in me forgives all people that have transgressed against me. Likewise, the infinite love in all people forgives me for transgressions that I committed against them. Everyone in thought and deed is blessed from this experience.*

Embrace Freedom

Now, release the situation and let go. As you let it go, think of a bird flying away from your presence high in the sky until it is no longer seen. Each time you venture to work and seemingly, unforgiving, overwhelming, or challenging situations appear, quickly bless them and let them go. Keep your thoughts moving . Infinite love has a way of melting even the coldest iceberg in supposedly unforgiving people. They may not show love towards you. Did you consider for a moment that somewhere in their lives that they do love something or someone? Infinite love is in all, and if you concentrate on that light within him/her, it will create a halt in the icy actions, reversing the situation to a spring/summer day. You may say some people are impossible; they appear to be loveless. Their disposition circles like sharks in the bay, waiting for an opportunity to strike its prey. Do not become fearful or believe this fallacy. *Everything* is changeable. Nothing is really, what it appears to be at that moment. See something good in that individual, and the good will come forth.

Perseverance, the Passage to Resolution

Some changes come with more patience and consistent focus. A snake trying to catch a bird does not swish around saying, "Here, birdie, birdie." He lies still in the sun, with focused eyes on that bird sitting on the branch. The snake maintains its focus for hours or days, however long, until the curious bird becomes enchanted. The snake draws the bird close in thoughts like a pin to a magnet. The snake then declares, "Game over." The snake has charmed the bird into submission by its intense and direct focus. The snake's thoughts have manifested into his heart's desire. Likewise, keep your eyes peeled on the good of the situation and do not deflect until the situation becomes amicable to your belief system or world. "Speak of excellent things." Speak and think happiness, joy, peace regarding the disturbing factor. Do not attempt forcing changes by running around complaining. Do not beg or plead with others to try to comprehend the situation, or struggle to advocate yourself with those who seemingly appear to have a misconstrued perception of you. Keep your mind focused on the change that you thirst for. Now is the time to smile a lot more, be high-spirited, and act as if you do not have a care in the world. Angels are all around advocating on your behalf. Who are your angels? All those wonderful thoughts you have incorporated about people will manifest into your world as the desires of your heart. Those angels (thoughts) will present themselves in people and actions in different aspects of your life,

FORGIVENESS—THE ART OF CLEANSING ONESELF/ONE'S WORLD

which will campaign on your behalf to bring your belief system to pass. Imagination is *everything*; whatever you believe to be the truth of yourself or situation will become a reflection in your active world.

I have met nurses who cannot seem to forgive anything. They exercise triumph out of constantly re-activating the volcanic experiences they created with others. The more you think and speak of the seemingly horrid situation, the more you create life like encounters of similar activities. I have seen countenances changed because of stored anger and un-forgiving hearts. Faces have become hardened, and smiles become a rarity. There is no displayed joy in the work area by such individuals as they have adopted such an acidic personality. To harbor hatred and anger towards any person or circumstance is to hinder one's progressive growth into the greater hemispheres in life.

Accept the "Cleaner Fish" in Your Life

In the ocean there is a fish called the "Cleaner Fish" or "Labroides Dimidiatus." This fish is only 10cm long, and its function is to remove parasites, wound tissues from large fish such as sharks, tuna, etc. The Cleaner Fish cleans the skin, mouth, and gills of the large fish, pulling anything from the skin and delicate organs such as the eye is uncomfortable. The large fish allows this treatment because it is healthy for its functionality and longevity of life. When the large fishes sees the Cleaner Fish, they change their colors to expose the parasites so the Cleaner Fish can remove them. Seemingly, difficult experiences in our lives are likened to the "Cleaner Fish" process. Entertain an attitude of openness and receptivity so that the cleaning/healing process can proceed without hindrance. View each experience as new growth, postulate each moment with forgiveness when it seems unkind or cruel, and be thankful for all. "In everything give thanks." When faced with challenging circumstances with people, those seemingly uncomfortable experiences are here to help us cultivate better attitudes of mind, to accentuate the enhancement of our greater good. Challenging people and circumstances travel our path to help us. They are indirectly beckoning us to bless them for the gift they gave us. It is for us to thank them and let them move forward into their greater good. We subconsciously choose them to collaborate with us in propelling us to be the kinder, smarter, stronger, patient, persistent, and wiser person. When people seemingly disappoint you, or seemingly annoy you, forgive them, and then thank them for the new enlightenment they have brought into your life. Release them in love, and they will move on and out of your life. Their deed have now been done in assisting you to become the better person you are.

Accommodating an acidic mind eventually influences the body to start a chemical reaction manifesting in diagnosis such as ulcers, colitis, arthritis, just to mention a few of the negative physiological changes that occurs in the body. Applying the law of forgiveness creates the homeostasis needed to balance our lives. We are physical and mental beings. Our thoughts become the things thought of. We do not have because we have not kept company with the things, which we sincerely desire. Here is where we have "sinned and have come short of the glory." The thoughts we think, how we feel about what we think manifest in our physical world. "Sinning" is only having the incorrect concept of the law. That is, the law is the creative process of the mind (subconscious mind). You sin when you think, feel, and participate in things that are less of the truth regarding you. To correct the flaw, one must completely abandon the agent perpetuating the emotion of anger, hatred, and unforgiveness.

Letting go of acidic embodiment is like inducing an opening in a carbuncle, allowing the purulent discharge to drain out. You will notice that as the dead cells exit, new tissue growth appears, giving room for the healing process. Letting go of unhealthy thoughts creates freedom of mind to receive and expand in mind and body. Replace unforgiving experiences with happy, healthy thoughts facilitates in redeeming one from sin, i.e., making a negative into a positive outcome. Repenting is changing of the mind, one's thought, or purpose, and in this case, replacing unforgiving thoughts with forgiveness. Forgiveness creates harmony with oneself and the situation. Create harmony within yourself by forgiving others. Expression of purpose illuminates as harmony dwells within. As long as you are at peace with yourself, the world will be at peace with you. When peace dwells within, you will see through the situation more clearly. Clear directions will guide your path as long as you believe that Divinity/Universal Life Source within you is enlightening your path.

Divine Order Aligns Your Outcome

Divine Order puts things in perspective, as it will guide you to the next step. Think of it as a ladder, providing you steps until you reach your destination. Your answer is always within, and it projects itself when the time is right. No one expects the student nurse to perform proficiently his/her clinical after 6 months of classroom work; neither do we expect the student to be adequately prepared to master the NCLEX(National Council Licensure Examination) with this minimum training. Divine Order guides us to each progression as soon as we master each step in the classroom of life. Before plants flower, they grow roots and branches with leaves. For that reason, Divine Order will guide your steps as you learn to practice forgiveness every day.

Your workload gets heavy at times, and then you may start

equating work with pay. *Do they pay me enough for all this work scope? Why do I always seem to get this difficult assignment?* Let us stop for a moment. As long as you work for an employer, he/she is supposed to take from you more in cash value than you get in paid wages. The employer's responsibility to you is to provide opportunities for growth in your career path that you may advance in given opportunities. Bless your work assignment, bless your job, and give thanks that it allows you to pay your expenses, and permits you to enjoy desired pleasures and meet your obligations. *You will not elevate to the next level of greatness in leadership or accumulate financial increase until you have acknowledged your present level as a blessing.* Heavy or difficult work assignments are inert triggers, propelling you to display the great leadership skills that were previously obscure. If your desire is for leadership, then always realize that "**an exceptional leader accepts responsibility, goes beyond the task at hand, and follows through to get it done properly**".

You are the resource nurse on the unit; the first assigned to precept new nurses. All other nurses come to you when in doubt. When it was time for a promotion for an assistant nurse manager, you applied. Human resources declined your application. The hospital hired someone new to the unit. Your knowledge and experience has again demanded you to orient the newly hired assistant nurse manager. When it was Nurse's Week, the colleagues you helped so many times nominated someone else less experienced or dedicated as "Nurse of the Week." Injustice has seemingly controlled your outcome. However, Divine Order is at work on your behalf. Take courage; no one is fighting against you. Accept the situation for what it is. Forgive yourself for thinking that your fellow teammates were unkind to you by passing over you. Inwardly seek their forgiveness. It is not time to start looking for the wrong in the situation. To question why, how, and when creates a multiplier for the experience. Be

FORGIVENESS—THE ART OF CLEANSING ONESELF/ONE'S WORLD

at peace with the situation. You will find out that Divine Order is in progress, creating possibilities for you. **"Missed opportunities are conduits for new prospects"**. Declare affirmations of strength in times when things appear complex. ***"Universal Life Source is creating and producing possibilities of abundant growth and empowerment for me right here and now."*** As always, be at peace with all things.

Write to an Angel Sometimes!

Meet unforgiving situations in your mind. Role-play the experience over in the pleasant way you would have wished it happened. Give thanks for the lessons you learned and new strength acquired. Sometimes you can apply writing a letter to your situation. Every experience has its own angel. Write a letter to the angel of the person, place, or thing.

Thank the Angel for the Healing of the Situation:

Dear angel of .... thank you for healing the relationship between me and ...., **etc.** Add and delete as necessary. Write your letter as often as you need to until you have peace with the moment regarding the situation. Keep your letter private. Then each time after, when confronted with thoughts of the incident, give thanks that, **In this situation, I am surrounded by Divine love and peace.**

Every day, in some way, we encounter an experience that creates that moment of anger, hatred, or frustration. To keep our flow in life constant, one must practice forgiveness at the opportune time of each incident, and at the closing of each day. Lay your burdens down. Like personal hygiene, forgiveness should become a daily habit. To initiate and practice forgiveness is to build ourselves a character that is needed to expand our visions and goals in life. As you release others in forgiveness, you relieve yourself of health issues and complex problems in your life. Spend time daily forgiving experiences of the past and present that you knowingly and unknowingly participated in.

Affirmation:
I release all burdensome experiences. Divine love dwelling within forgives and heals me of wrong thinking and action.

When you practice affirmations of forgiveness, think of a high wall crumbling to the ground. Forgiveness demolishes emotional walls, letting them become passages to cross over into one's better good. Forgiveness will affect your life as a cool bath on a hot day, invigorating and relaxing. Remember, when circumstances appear too overwhelming, try the forgiveness therapy. Somewhere hidden in the subconscious is a retained thought of hostility, hatred, or anger regarding past event that is blocking your flow to receiving the blessings that Divinity patiently awaits to pour into your life. You may become offended, hurt, frustrated, or displeased because of people's words and actions. You allowed yourself to attach an unhappy emotion to these actions because you did not recognize that this was a part of your growing process. Understand that **Divinity/Universal Life Source is in all things, and the displeasure brought on by the actions of others is only a directory to your Divine Purpose in life.**

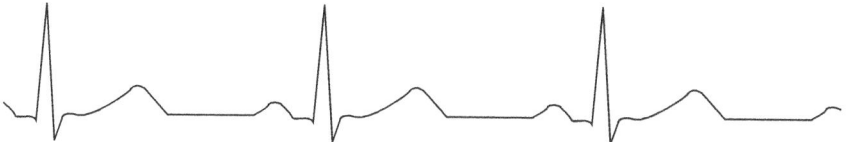

Chapter 4

The Law of Nonresistance

Do not fight with people, institutions, or circumstances. The little fire that you kindle today will only escalate into a huge inferno tomorrow. Water will always find its outlet, even if you try to block its path. The Law of Non-Resistance is when faced with opposing forces, instead of participating; withdraw your energy by not chipping into the negative situation. As you ignore the inflammatory situation, it will cease to extract your energy for attention and dissipate into nothingness. "Resist the devil and he will flee from thee"(Mass of thoughts that have been built up through many generations of earthly experiences . . . termed human personality.)The devil (evil) is only the adverse thought that creates opposition to the truth of your Divine Nature. Your divine nature is joy, happiness, prosperity, success, wealth, and fulfillment. Go within and create the opposite of what is happening around you. If you have to respond, speak to the situation as you would like the conversation to be. By entertaining your desired state of the situation, it deletes the energy of the opposition, which will bring about the best in the person involved or change the course of things to work in your favor.

Did a doctor or a fellow coworker call you an idiot before everyone? After caring for a patient with all your professionalism possible and giving the best care ever, did the relative of that same patient come and say, "You are incompetent, and you do not know what you are doing! In fact, I need a new nurse to care for my loved one!" Your first response is to put that someone in his or her place and set the record straight. Everyone is looking at you. In everyone's mind around you, you hear the voices saying, "Are you going to let him or her get away with that?" Somewhere we learned that when faced with an opposing force we should immediately fight back. "Nip it in the bud," they say. Anything else and you will be labeled as "soft, stupid, or easy." You think that you have to retaliate to prove that you are not what people say you are. Did you ever notice that in challenging situations, the more you fight back, the more the hostility escalates like an inferno? Did you realize that physically and emotionally, energy becomes depleted in these types of warfare, and usually nothing gets accomplished? In the "battle of the wits," we only create disharmony within ourselves, and in creating disharmony we eliminate our good from coming to us.

Resistance creates constant self-medication of the thing that angers you. The subconscious will now re-create more of the feeling felt and picture imagined. For every event, fall not into the mist of the illusion that it creates. Immediately re-create in your mind what you want the outcome to be. Undo the message of the messenger who declared the negative on the expected outcome. Creation lies awake on the inside, ready and waiting to bring to pass your ideals. Stay in the place called "there." "There" is where imagination is active, and your ideals are actively in motion. Your subconscious mind is asking you to "tarry here and watch with me." Stay a while longer with your ideals and wait for the manifestation of your good.

There is no need to defend the truth about yourself or circumstances. **Truth is divinity in confinement, which always reveals itself during unscheduled moments.** Applying the Law of Resistance daily is exercising mastery of self, displayed when we are

THE LAW OF NONRESISTANCE

not contentious or actively fighting to prove ourselves right; it is living above troublesome situations and not becoming encumbered by one's condition. "Let every man be swift to hear, slow to speak, slow to wrath." Remember always that life's challenges are filled with lessons and hidden blessings, so accept all with gracious thankfulness.

Whatever someone thinks about you is a representation of his or her own judgment. Their perception of you is a creation from their own ideology. You should not waste time and energy exerting yourself to receive acceptance by physical endeavors; you will only create an apocalypse of your own creation, catapulting to dissension in the process. That which someone labels you as is only a reflection of that person. **People only identify in you what is already in them. We are mirrors of each other.** One only meets himself in others in his daily interactions and exchanges. If you do not like something in someone else, it is time to correct the flaw in yourself, as those you meet come to remind you of the weakness within. Take note and start the repair work in forgiveness and affirmations of good. There is no need to be angry with the next person, as you will only be creating obstacles for your changes towards your greater good. "Why behold the mote in thy brother's eye . . . consider not the beam in your own eye." Correct the flaw that presents itself to you within yourself, and simultaneously, the highest good will reciprocate from others to you.

In challenging situations, go within and affirm your divinity of what you want out of the situation. Work with only that, which is comfortable and acceptable to your divine nature. Go with the flow and ride the tides. Believe in yourself. There is unlimited strength within to sustain you; do not give allowance to the dictates of the external environment, which seek to lure you from the ideal you picture in your mind. Always remember that the subconscious accepts the idea that you acknowledge as the truth of you and happily reproduces more of the same.

When you participate in actions that are not a part of your Divine Nature, you create resistance to righteousness (righteousness as in the things that are right for you). With resistance, you harbor and create disharmony in the subconscious and deny self of victorious situations. Disharmony is feeding your subconscious state with information and feelings that are not in alignment with the superconscious state (the part of us that wants us expressed to our highest self). Divinity in us only wants us to achieve our ultimate good in all situations.

With every obstacle there is always a way to work around it to allow for your continued path to your good. If you should plant some seeds in a stony path, you will notice that the seed spouts around the rock to allow the plant to express itself in growth. The seed does not try to push the rocks out of the way to grow. The seed applies the Law of Non-Resistance in its tender years by growing around the rock; it does not expel its energy in trying to move the rock out of the way. Chances are, if it did, it would die in the process. The seed found the path of least resistance to expression.

Instead of dispelling one's energy in moving obstacles, apply the Law of Non-Resistance and greet every situation with peace, seek the safe path around it, and continue your walk to expressing your good. As you walk in the comfort of knowing that, you are not alone, peace will enlighten your path to success and victory, and you will become stronger every day. "Bless them that persecute you: bless and curse not." When you extend thoughts of blessings and goodness towards those who seem difficult, you have immediately eliminated vacancy for negative growth. You have now contacted your superconscious state and informed it that you are at one with the Divine Good in yourself. Becoming aligned with one's Divine Good attracts the Divine Good in people or situations. In attracting the highest good in all, you have created the path of least resistance to your challenges. In practicing the Law of Non Resistance, it guides you into grounding self, enhances self-actualization, and deflates incoming darts of malicious intent.

No Person Can Deny Your Good!

Did you ever have someone in authority threaten to dismiss you from your job or threaten to write a negative report about you? Do not start attaching emotions of fear or anxiety to their spoken words; desist from becoming a receptacle for fear mongering. Eliminate sleepless nights and thoughts of how life will change without a job. Act as if the spoken words are unimportant. **Things die for the lack of attention. Words become powerful only when we accept them as truth in our minds, thus, giving permission to our subconscious to create them into life events.** No one can deny you of your good: even if it appears that, they may be making leaps and bounds to your demise, there will be no victory gained as long as you do not accept their truth as your truth. Get over people's personalities and start seeing the principle for which they exist. Your connection is to their Divine Nature (intelligence) which came as a light to your path for growth and expansion.

Managers and institutions are not your source of supply. Divinity within is the source of all creative substance and will supply all your needs. Keep your mind on the source of your supply. Remind yourself of your creative process by decreeing: *"I am created in Divine Design. Divinity in me expresses in full manifestation. I am open, ready, and receive the highest and best that divinity now pours*

into me. If you see your manager or institution as your source of supply, then you have started "idol worshiping," believing that they are the sole provision of your source of supply, rather than merely one of the contributory factors of the vast resources of the universe. Divinity within you wants you to acclaim your supply from within. "Thou shall have no other gods before me." Acknowledging the Divinity within opens you to a continuous flow of abundance in your life that no one can hinder you from receiving. Complete trust in people, places, and things short circuits one's supply. We should trust in the infinite divinity within for everything we need. We limit our supply when we look to an outward existence for the source of our supply.

Did you experience job termination? Do you feel angry? Release the anger and frustration. You should not become remorseful about it. This will only re-create more of the same and continue the trend in your current experiences. As long as you keep anger, hatred, and retaliation hidden in your consciousness, you will never be able to see the light to the new path in life created just for you. It is now time to shift your thoughts from the effects of what is happening around you and reunite with the divinity within by affirming, ***"I am Divinity in action with unlimited possibilities."*** Stay in this thought, because if you give into the fear, you would have surrendered your power to the given situation and become servant to it. Every servant must obey its master, and if fear becomes your master, then you will be functioning in the spiraling effects of fear. **No one can take your good unless you give away your power by succumbing to the fear of the threat propagated.** Reverse the process of allowing others to control you. Refocus your thoughts on the Divinity within, who is the true supplier of all your needs. Divine Source, the all-provider of unlimited abundance, will provide for your unlimited opportunities of good.

THE LAW OF NONRESISTANCE

Never for one moment should you accommodate fear. It inhibits your strength, as it keeps your vision in a state of stasis. To accommodate fear with your goal is to eliminate your opportunity for growth towards the vision of progression. Always remind yourself that Divinity dwelling within will work out every detail in divine order, systematically and conclusively. Like glue to paper, your only job is to hold on to the vision or picture in your mind. Never give anyone or any situation permission to rob you of your belief system.

The termination of your job is Divinity in action, creating for you new opportunities. The lessons in your former position are now complete. You have passed the test. No student should stay in kindergarten when it is time to be promoted to first grade. You have outgrown your current circumstances, and it is now time to move to the next level. Accept this as good. **With acceptance comes enlightenment and elevation.** Change is good. Be prepared for expansion and new responsibilities. There will be new opportunities to explore. *One never knows his or her full potential until engaged in new explorations.* Divinity is only propelling you to your highest good, and it comes in all forms. Bless your experiences, give thanks for all that you learned and achieved, and keep going forward.

Add Honey to seemingly Lemon Situations

During unpleasant exchanges, try injecting some praise and laughter in the situation. "A merry heart makes a cheerful countenance". Give praise to the person about their achievement, looks, or their performance of work done. Praising someone connects with the Divine Nature in that individual which immediately recognizes itself in you. It is very easy to be nice when things are going well. Try giving some praise in troublesome situations. Try offering something complimentary when you have a heavy work assignment. After completing the night shift of no break time, standing for most of the shift, now that it has ended and you think that you can now leave to get some much-needed rest, you suddenly hear that a staff meeting will take place and you have to stay an extra hour. *Now* is the time to think of a happy moment to take you to a happier state; to lift your spirit to a higher elevation that will connect you to the superconscious or ideal state within. When we connect ourselves to our higher state of being, we begin to change our perspective on life as it happens around us. Connecting self to the Divinity within creates changes for better situations.

Applying praise to a troublesome environment is not so much an action for others, but it is a source of comfort and strength to aid you in extracting the good of the situation and thus, receive the blessings therein. It ultimately creates the change you desire in your environment. Praising situations gives you freedom from the stressful environment. Expressing praise and thanksgiving in tumultuous situations freezes the action of negative stimuli and releases positive atoms, creating the change desired and deserved. **Every challenge is a catalyst in action calling for your insightful understanding.** *Give praise and thanks for the challenge because when you activate praise, your Divine Nature takes notice and brings clarity to your vision.* When your vision becomes clear, you will understand the battle of your current circumstance.

In every situation, give thanks always. Profusion of the mind with praise detonates outcomes of happy and healthy lifestyles. Praise is like the thoroughfare leading to the better good of all. Praise is like a garden of beautiful flowers, appealing to sight and smell, picturesque and fragrant. When you speak the good of and into a situation, you create the good that will effectively summon the best of the circumstances. This creates for you tranquility and brings to pass that which is the greater good of all.

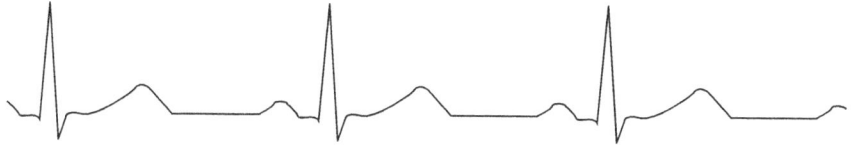

Chapter 5

My Words Are My Destiny

Your words either build you up or create a destructive path for your life. We have now understood that we are solely responsible for the outcomes in our lives by the words we speak, the thoughts we think, with whatever emotion we attach to the thought and spoken word. "In the beginning was the word, the word was with God, and the word was God." For every experience, it first began with a word.

The spoken word expressed in our conscious experiences is accepted in the subconscious as the experience you desired. The subconscious only reproduces more of what it is given. It does not have the ability to change anything, and that, my friend, "has become flesh," the experience that evolved in one's daily experience. "Trapped with the words of your mouth." You create your own entrapment by the words that you speak and conversations that you entertain. Think before you act, and when you act, speak only words that will influence a positive asset in the whole scheme of things. As you participate in daily affairs, your subconscious is reproducing the input of all activities.

Heal Self First

In an effort to heal others, heal yourself first. You heal yourself by taking into account every word spoken and every action taken. The seed you plant will only produce fruits of its own kind. Everything that you desire is within reach. It only seems distant because you have not been abiding with the "Law of Mind": thinking and speaking the desired state of the circumstances. When you speak and think the desired state in all circumstances, it magnetizes you towards the superconscious state (the perfect state of man that gave you the desire of a better self or circumstance) and the state of being that we were created to function in. It is like the clothes that always fit right. Your future only seems to be at a distance because you are not working with "The Law of Mind." Get in tune with "The Law of Mind" and this genie action will accelerate the future self to the present self. You create your own "Laws of Mind" by the thoughts you think daily. This conscious thinking is conveyed to our subconscious, which, in turn, processes the thought, becoming the law out pictured in our world.

No one has the power to deny you of your good . . . but you. The power of creation is in your hands. What you do with it is up to you. Your world is creation in expression; an out picturing of your words and thoughts. Whatever situation you have found yourself caged in is only a result of a previous thought. Unchain you mind and speak into life words of liberation to change your circumstances as this will be the only lasting passage to change. Progression is the nature of man; within you is an expansive capacity waiting for expression. There are no failures, only directives for changes to facilitate progressive growth.

Start outlining your goals in life. Every builder creates a blueprint before he builds. Let your goals be your guide to change. Speak and think into the desired good. See yourself there. Do not become concerned of how to make the journey. Fill yourself with goodness, praise, and thanksgiving. Day by day, things will get better and better. Give thanks for everything, for the little changes as well as the big ones. Expect the good, aim high always. Accommodate happiness in your world daily.

Did you notice that no one wants to stay in a morgue? It is always cold and silent. Your world becomes morgue like when one is constantly saddened and hardened by situations. A saddened countenance repels and wards off others from around us, including your prosperous moments. Each time thoughts of emotions of sadness come, think that if they are entertained, you will be closing the door for a happy moment. No one wants to give up happiness voluntarily. Live for each moment as if it is the *only* moment. Everything will work itself out. Keep on the brighter side today and tomorrow will be golden. Anticipate that your good will harvest in your lifetime as you live and breathe each day. Detach yourself from troublesome people, places, and things. As you look and seek for the best in all, the best will also look for you. Believe in yourself; believe in the words that you speak, that they will come to pass. "Heaven and earth shall pass away, but my words shall not pass away." One's greatest asset is knowing that we are the authority to the words we speak. We breathe life into them as we speak. The spoken word creates form, unleashing their actions into our lives. Use your powers to saturate your life with all the good you so deserve. Your word is the center of your creation.

Speak and stand in the truth of your belief system; refrain from denying the truth of your spoken word. **Thoughts of denial of one's good, induces an abortion to the intent of one's creation**. Many people say they want to be successful and wealthy, but within, they deny this because maybe someone told them they did not deserve to be that way, or someone said it was pious to be poor, or by thinking that this is not their path in life. If such statements were ever spoken to your belief system, it is time for an exorcism of such thoughts. They are impediments towards your good. **What you mold in the clay of thought will become the picturesque display in your world** *for all to see.*

For everyday, for everyone that you identify as a rung on the ladder to your success, give thanks for all. Remember, some of these helpers may not come in packages that are appealing to the eyes or ears. In focusing on your goal of successful expression, you acknowledge everyone in your path as you walk upwards and onwards. Acknowledge the principle of the person or situation, not the personality or presentation.

Chapter 6

You Are Not Alone

Our conscious, subconscious, and superconscious state of being are always with us. They are frequently spoken in whispers or expressed in a loud outburst that "God is with us always." As creative beings, deciding our experiences in the thoughts we think, and actions taken will display that "God is with us always"."God", your creative expression, out pictured from the subconscious world will be for you or against you, depending on the instructions given to the subconscious. You can only receive a result or by-product of your initial investment.

Faced with extraneous situations, one sometimes feels isolated from people, places, and things. You are not alone. The negative effects will attempt to overwhelm you, as they constantly demand your attention. What kind of attention are you going to give to that energy that is constantly charging? *Now* is the time to decree peace to the storm that swirls so heavily around you. Your superconscious state is always with you and holds the truth of you with the desired outcome. To have the desired outcome, it calls for you to decree peace in the current experience and focus on the desired outcome. This is the time to hold on to thoughts and pictures of the end of the circumstances.

LORETTA L. BONNICK, RN

The following are neutralizing affirmations to challenging situations. As you develop strength in self and circumstances, you will start developing your own words of strength and positive replacement for negative thoughts and actions. Patience is a virtue; some things take longer to dissipate, as we have spent a lifetime learning negative responses to circumstances. Constantly affirm positive thoughts daily. Write them on cue cards; keep them in places where you can see them as a reminder to the truth of you. I have included a few suggestions for comfort and growth. Practiced daily, it gets better with time and take note how they create changes in your seemingly challenging circumstances.

AFFIRMATIONS

To create Peace in Situations
I am peace. Peace transcends my soul and all my circumstances are veiled in tranquility. I release this fear of .... and magnetize to myself joy, peace, success, and prosperity.

If you ever feel loveless, confused about your existence:
I am love. I am destined for greatness. I am a light to the world around me. Universal Life Source is always with me, guiding my every footstep for every decision made for every moment of my existence. I am love

Did you get displaced from your job or were denied a promotion:
I learn everyday from my experiences. There is good in everything that happens around me. Universal Life Source is my guide to understanding and advancement of my greater good. Endless opportunities are created for me. I am now guided by Universal Life source to the next step of advancement in my purpose. I give thanks for my answer as it is here with me always.

YOU ARE NOT ALONE

Have you lost hope or do you feel a sense of helplessness
Universal love surrounds me and is in all that is happening around me. Universal love is the life source that removes everything that is not of my divine nature . Today, I am thankful that I am guided to right answers and my true purpose in life.

Needing guidance:
Universal Life Source is my beginning and my ending. All the answers I desire are within me. Thank you Universal Life Source for bringing the right answers at the right time. With thanksgiving and joy, I now receive the abundance of good that is mine...

Restoring health: Does not matter what it feels, sounds, or looks like:
I assert every cell in my body healthy. I thank Universal Life Source for its unending substance of supply. From this unlimited supply of substance, every unhealthy cell is replaced with healthy cells. I bless my body for the wonderful work it does every day, and my body functions in perfect harmony.

When hurtful situations cling to your thoughts and demand revenge:
Everything that is not part of my divine nature is released from my being. I release all hidden hatred, resentment ,biased and unloving thoughts. I now embrace happiness, peace and joy. I open myself to the Universal Life Source of good in every aspect of my life.

When feeling unloved, abandoned and alone, decree:
I am Infinite Love. Infinite love engulfs me. I am attracted to people who are loved and are happy. Every day I am happy as I love myself and others love me. I am purpose, I make others happy and others make me happy.

Are you holding on to toxic situations, people, places, *or things* seemingly unforgiveable people or situations:
I thank you for the encounter or experience. Divine love that dwells in me forgives you and the divine love in you forgives me. I do not hold on the experience but I release you as you release me. We both walk to our greater good from this experience and divine love surrounds us both.

Do you believe that others are more successful than you or do you think that you never have enough? Affirm:
I am happy for life. I am grateful for my achievements and life lessons. Everyday I learn new ways to make myself better and better. I am thankful for successful people as they inspire me towards my greater good. Universal Life Source has unlimited supply of substance that provides for me daily.

Grieving for the Loss of a Loved One; Affirm:
Our life together in life was special. I learnt from you and I am thankful for the moments we spent together. We have completed our time together and I now release you into your greater good.

Believe that which you speak or pray will manifest in the faith of what you feel and see: Affirm:
I am thankful that my words spoken will now manifest in my world. I now rest as my creation now becomes visible.

Practice prayer (affirmations) daily. As situations change, continue to practice as your good becomes better and your better becomes the best. Keep your prayers simple and record your requests and the answers as they come. Believe what you are requesting. If you believe that you have received, you certainly shall have that which you asked for. There is no need to beg for anything; it is through prayer i.e. (the belief of the truth regarding your situation) that you will process your better good. Keep your minds filled with the positive outlook of life to eliminate complexes of Wandering Pacemakers, PVC's(Premature Ventricular Contractions), Junctional beats, PEA,s (Premature Atrial Complexes), or Asystole like events from your active world. Keeping life in the Normal Sinus Rhythm mode maintains the calm and, keeps one grounded to focus, think, and act right in every given situation, thus, producing the ideal outcome of one's heart desires.

Why I Wrote This Book

I worked for an agency in New Jersey staffing several hospitals on a per-diem and sometimes on a contractual basis. I continued this work for 5 years, showing up to work during snowstorms when regular staff could not go to work, staying extra hours when necessary without the benefit of overtime pay, always getting to work on time. One day I got an e-mail saying that I was terminated. It was stated that dismissal was based on the grounds of me not producing a yearly medical on time. The reasons told for dismissal were numerous. Among them were that I did not return my yearly medical. Another reason was that I was loud and boisterous. At the time of termination, I did have my medical in my possession, which the employer was not aware of.

Coincidentally, 3 months before this event, I noticed that there was a "Houdini" effect on some of the hours I worked and documented on the time sheets submitted. There were always questionable doubts regarding the actual hours worked and how much was disbursed on one's check. I called the office several times, and when there was no response to my inquiries, I wrote a very nice letter highlighting discrepancies I found. After several reminders, reimbursement was eventually given for some portions. It seemed peculiar that dismissal came 3 months after this incident for other inconsequential activities.

LORETTA L. BONNICK, RN

For over a year, I made several applications, but without success, for a new nursing job. I even found out that my previous employer's story changed to say that I was a war-like employee. I received outstanding performance and professional references from the facilities I worked with, one year after assignment completion.

I thank my previous employer for being so creative in building walls for me. It was through this seemingly challenging period in my life that I withdrew from within and penned the contents of this book. Out of the ash and mud grows the beautiful Lotus flower. There is good in all things, so maintain your patience, and most of all, believe that there is a greater expression within that needs to be manifested. Imagination is everything. You can create your outcome. Compel your good by decreeing blessings to all things. Bless your home, car, clothes, pen, or book, just to name a few. Lighten up; add some fun to your world. Words of blessings just make you a more positive person. As you bless, your actions are calling out to the best in that thing or person. Blessings invoke the Divinity or God-like aspect of the object of interest and awaken the realm of the invisible world. Take note of the good results that returns to you.

It is my heart's desire that by reading this book, you will be motivated to a higher state of self-accomplishment. May you find joy and fun in your function. May you have peace, blessings, prosperity, and fulfillment as you walk daily in your destined path, completing your purpose in this lifetime.

Blessings, Health and Peace . . .

References

Bible, King James Version

www.ingramcontent.com/pod-product-compliance
Lightning Source LLC
Chambersburg PA
CBHW051717040426
42446CB00008B/936